Reader reviews for *Don't Be An Asshole!*

The preface is so well written, that alone is worth the price of the book. If you travel for a living and all your friends and family think a traveling job is a "luxurious, jet-setting lifestyle." buy them this book. They will get a dose of your reality and a good laugh too. Then keep reading because it gets better and funnier. — **S. Romer**

I couldn't put it down. I believe that reading this book should be a prerequisite for graduating high school followed by a book report on what was learned. — **Mike B.**

What a witty, truthful, well written book. The illustrations will have you on the floor rolling over. I agree with Mike B. Should be required reading. — **Guitarman**

Great book ...funny well worth the price. After halfway back on a red eye from LA, I had finished it and the guy next to me asked to read some for the rest of the flight. He could not stop laughing. — **Rock316**

This book seriously made me laugh from beginning to end. I love the way it's written and it's all soo true. I appreciated the approach the writer took with the subject and how he used a sore topic and flipped it into a common sense, light-hearted approach to the crazy world we live in. – **Paul F.**

Holy Cow!!! This had to be the funniest download I have got yet. The best part it is Free!!! Probably won't be for too much longer.Great read and a must have!!! – **Toad**

One of the funniest and also most informative books I've ever read. If you need to kill some time, or just entertain yourself to no end, then this book is for you. Worth more than its weight! – **Chris G.**

ISBN-13: 978-1481809191
ISBN-10: 1481809199

Visit us on the web!

www.dontbeanassholebook.com

Table of Contents

I.　Acknowledgements

I would like to first acknowledge my wife of nearly 20 years for putting up with someone who can at times be the biggest asshole of them all, me. I would also like to thank her for taking care of just about everything else while I worked on this project. You rock babe!

Second, I would like to acknowledge my sister from another mister, Joanne Mckenzie, who I never knew before a few months ago but could very well the female version of myself. She contributed a lot of written material for the book and helped keep me sane throughout the process. She's as funny as she is talented. Thank you Jo.

Last but not least I would like to thank Shayne Lloyd for taking my cryptic notes and transforming them into wonderful works of art. He provided all of the illustrations for the book and did a bang-up job.

I would also like to acknowledge a great friend who I hadn't talked to in nearly twenty years. We reconnected this past year on Linked In and in the few months since he has donated ridiculous amounts of his time and valuable experience to help me reach my personal goals, including showing me how to take ideas like this book and other products and turn them into real things. Thanks Paul.

Lastly I would like to thank all of the assholes in the world, without which this book would not be possible.

II.   Preface

My experience with assholes came to a head while working a job that required me to travel extensively. You simply have not lived until you travel by air on a near constant basis for an extended period of time. In my case it was 7 years. My friends and family thought I was so lucky to be able to "see the world". They viewed it as a luxurious, jet-setting lifestyle. There were three main fallacies in their way of thinking. One, I didn't travel internationally, just throughout the US, so I didn't see the world. Two, when you travel for work (at least for this particular job) this is what you see: airport, interstate, work site, hotel, interstate, airport...and repeat. I was by myself so meals were always alone and anything interesting I did happen upon were only shared with myself which kind of takes the fun out of it. Three, there is nothing luxurious about air travel anymore. Even when you hit elite status with all the air carriers and fly first class on every flight, it still sucks. At that point you're pretty much surrounded by people who have the same work schedule you do and they're all miserable too. The best part of flying was just getting to my seat and listening to music or reading a book and zoning out for a few hours. Now with most flights offering WiFi, even that's going away. Most flight attendants seemed two steps away from going completely bat-shit crazy on everyone on the plane (and to be honest if I had to deal with so many assholes on a daily basis I wouldn't be far behind them).

Air travel is a good example of fertile ground that allows for the rapid growth of assholes. I know for a fact because when I started travelling I was an excited, happy-go-lucky sort of chap with a cheery tune in my head and a spring in my step. After a year I was a miserable son of a bitch who hated everyone first and asked questions second. The experience wasn't completely without its merits though. It did give me an enormous appreciation for non-assholes. Those that in the face of asshole-ish-ness (???) managed to hold their ground and remain decent people. It also gave me the time-consuming yet cathartic past time of identifying assholes in the world and documenting their behaviors and habits.

That is how the idea of this book came to me and that is when I started mentally filing away all of my run-ins with assholes. The overabundance of assholes you have to deal with from all walks of life and in every part of the journey while simply trying to get from point A to Point B is staggering. The assholes online or on the phone when you buy your tickets, the assholes on the road on the way to the airport, the assholes in the parking lot, on the elevator, in line, at the ticket counter, on the tram, at security, on the plane...DAAAAHHHHH!

Now, before I go any further let me just say I am certainly not perfect and have had more than my share of asshole moments. I am positive that some people I know in my life right now, maybe most of them, think I'm an asshole. I'd like to say it's because someone else's asshole behavior TURNED me into one but there have been situations where it was all my own doing. At one point or another in our lives we've all been guilty of it. It can be part of human nature; but some people just seem to cherish that sort of behavior way more than others. They revel in it. They ENJOY being assholes. It's mainly those types of people that inspired me to write a book on the topic. I find it fascinating in a weird kind of way. Who are these people and why do they act like that? Do they know they're assholes? Do they care?

During our little journey through asshole kingdom I'll go into what I've identified as the 7 "Types of Assholes" and then break it down by situations and places where assholes are typically found. Strategically placed in between some chapters are little "breathers" I call *Inspiration Intermissions* where you can find out about someone who did something really nice. I put these in so you don't get all heated and stab someone in the face. There's the occasional tip on how to handle certain assholes as well as some great visual representations of assholes by a talented cartoonist. One thing to note is there were no scientific studies done here. No lab experiments, no behavioral interviews, no psychiatric screenings. Everything in this book is based purely on my own observations and opinions...and you know what they say about opinions.

III.   Introduction

Why are there so many assholes in the world? It's a question I've asked myself and heard others ask many times over. Who are these people we label so freely? Are they part of some underground network of assholes that meet bi-monthly to come up with ways to make "the rest of us" miserable? Are they a new breed of terrorist hell-bent on systematically breaking our spirit slowly over time until we've lost all hope for humanity? If so, some might argue it's working...or has already worked.

If you don't know what I'm talking about, welcome to Earth. Allow me to provide a brief example of an asshole encounter: Maybe YOU just got promoted. Maybe YOU just won the lottery. Maybe YOUR significant other surprised you with "a little something extra" this morning and you're just tip-toeing through the tulips all the way to work. Meanwhile, Johnny Sourpuss in the car next to you just found out his home loan was denied, is running late for a job he can't stand and is seriously considering a fresh start in Mexico. The two of you don't know each other and don't particularly care to. You're driving along wondering how anything can spoil your day. You signal to change lanes in front of Johnny. There's plenty of room. As you start to move over, Johnny floors it and gets right on the tail of the car in front of him blocking your way. You end up getting behind Johnny and he slows down dramatically. You try to pass him and he speeds up. Is this a string of coincidences or is Johnny just a plain asshole? In this particular case, Johnny is having a rotten day and probably just wants to take it out on someone. Either way your blood pressure just skyrocketed and you're not as chipper as you were a few moments before. You may even feel inclined to act out on someone else yourself. "Paying it forward" can be done in a negative way too. You're just another unfortunate casualty of the actions of an asshole.

Now, there are lots of examples of people and situations that highlight asshole behavior in this book. So much so that while writing this book I found myself getting angrier and angrier, thinking about all the assholes I've dealt with over the years. Then a funny thing happened; I started feeling like a major asshole myself! For feeling compelled to identify and log behavior patterns and actions I so liberally label as "being an asshole". I also started wondering how my readers might feel after finishing a book that's solely about people who are assholes; probably not so good. They would probably be in bad moods themselves, thinking about all the times THEY were affected by assholes. I really had to come up with something to change that since my intent for this book was never to make people disgusted with themselves or with the people around them and leave them feeling negative towards society as a whole. My goal was to provide a funny and entertaining piece of work that everyone could relate to and in the end, maybe make some people more aware of how their actions might affect others.

So as you're reading this, keep your tongues firmly planted in your cheeks and have your grains of salt at the ready because that is how I wrote it and that's the mentality I want everyone to take from it.

IV.   Types of Assholes

It's not easy trying to lump people into tidy, all-encompassing groups but this is my stab at it. Nearly everyone will have differing opinions of what types of assholes there should and should not be in this list. As the saying goes, "opinions are like assholes; everyone has one and it usually stinks." Not YOUR opinion. I value YOURS. You bought this book. I'm talking about the idiots who didn't.

I came up with seven "types". I put a lot of thought into this and I think they cover all of them. After the types of assholes we jump right into all the different kinds of assholes you may encounter in the wild in "Assholes All Around Us". For fun you can decide what you think is the best "type" of asshole that corresponds to the asshole examples listed, but you really don't have to.

Note:
To illustrate the "types of assholes" I've listed, I provided some...well...illustrations to help drive the point home. To simplify things even further, I came up with a central theme which is simply "a group of kids getting ice cream"...

#1) The True or Certified Asshole:

The worst of the worst. These are the unapologetic, 24/7 douchebags of society that can make life miserable if you let them. They KNOW they're assholes and they LIKE BEING assholes. If you had asked them as children what they wanted to be when they grew up they would have said "Asshole. I want to be an asshole!" There's nothing you can really do with these people. They are unredeemable. Don't even count on the fact that they have sad lives and that's why they're acting out. They have great lives because they're doing exactly what they love...being assholes. Just identify them quickly and stay away at all costs. If you can't stay away (think coworkers/bosses/family members) just remember this: The only strength they have is your weakness. Don't care about what they do and they'll have no real power.

*Little Becky here just smashed all the other kids' cones to the ground and couldn't be happier. Why?
Because she's an asshole.*

"Certified's" LOVE the work they do!

#2) The Uneducated Asshole:

These are the people who are assholes because they just don't know any better. Growing up they were never taught how not to be an asshole. The bright side is for these people this book doesn't just serve as a tongue-in-cheek, comedic take on society but more of a step by step guide on what they need to do to change their ways. There is still hope for this type of asshole.

Simon isn't trying to be an asshole; he just thinks
his litter looks better on the pavement.

#3) The Inadvertent Asshole:

These are people who are unintentionally assholes at certain moments. Unlike the uneducated assholes, they know the difference between right and wrong. They aren't trying to be assholes but were caught off guard for whatever reason and did an asshole thing temporarily. You can identify these types easily as they will usually immediately apologize for their asshole behavior. An example of this would be someone who misjudges the timing in traffic and cuts you off or pulls out in front of you almost causing a wreck but then they give you the "I'm sorry wave". This is the most favorable type of asshole.

In her haste to get her own ice cream, Cindy <u>inadvertently</u> makes Billy drop his to the floor.

To make up for her actions, she brings Billy back another one. Awww, I can't stay mad at you...

#4) The Spiteful Asshole:

This is a kind of hybrid asshole that combines the True Asshole with the Inadvertent Asshole. Another name for them could be Werewolf Asshole, Hulk Asshole or Jekyll and Hyde Asshole. Normally they're fine, upstanding members of society but when they get angry because something bad happened to them like they lost money on the big game or they found a fingernail in their oatmeal, they want to take it out on anyone and everyone. Their day took a turn for the worst and they want to make sure everyone around them has the same experience. The feeling of wrecking someone else's good time is healing to them. During this "episode" the best thing to do is give them a wide berth and by all means don't try to make them feel better. Just leave them the Hell alone before you get sucked in and get hurt. They'll go back to normal if just given some time.

Charley's ice cream accidentally falls to the floor.

To retaliate against life's sudden and unforeseen cruelties, he knocks Tom's down as well. THAT'LL teach him for being there!

#5) The Default Asshole:

These people are not really assholes themselves but are forced to do asshole things because of their position or lot in life (i.e. middle management, probation officers, attorneys, parents, some teachers perhaps...you get the gist). You can't really hold them responsible for their actions unless they REALLY enjoy being the asshole they are forced to be. It's those types of people that make it on this list.

Rita likes ice cream as much as the next person, but she's got a job to do. Sorry kiddies, no verbal warning for you.

#6) Old Assholes:

This is probably one of the sadder examples of asshole. I almost didn't include this one because I think most of them deserve a pass on this list. These are generally senior citizens who have either become assholes over time because they've dealt with so many assholes during their lives or are assholes because things just don't work the way they used to and new pains surface on an almost daily basis. You can't get too upset with this type because no one past the age of 21 ever said "I wish I was older!" HOWEVER, the True or Certified Asshole types (described before) get old too and they've just been assholes their whole lives so they get no sympathy from me.

George can't eat ice cream anymore for a whole plethora of reasons. It sucks to get old...

...unless you're an asshole.

#7) Young Assholes:

Wooo baby! These are the profanity yelling, stereo blasting, graphic Tee wearing, scene making, bass thumping, binge drinking, lie telling, aggressive driving, weight lifting, annoying haircut having, in your face, no holds barred little punk bastards we ALL love to hate! The only caveat? Most of us were just like them when we were younger too. These can almost be lumped in with the uneducated assholes because most of them just don't know any better yet.

Young assholes just do what feels good at the time no matter the consequences. Being young and stupid allows them to embrace their asshole endeavors.

V.   Assholes All Around Us

The next several chapters contain examples of some of the more favored situations and gathering places of the North American asshole. Though every effort has been made to make this list as comprehensive as possible, there are simply far too many types of assholes in the world to accurately document them all. This list is not by any means an all-inclusive one and should not be used as such.

1)   Religious Assholes

GOOD GOD! How did religion get to the top of the heap? I must be brave or stupid and I'm not exceptionally brave so I'm gonna keep this one brief.

Sooooo, onto the totally minefield-free landscape that is the subject of religion.

You probably think I'm going to bash all the nice folks who just can't seem to stop themselves from trying to save humanity one soul at a time. Well I will in a moment but there's another group out there that's quickly becoming just as annoying. The Atheists. What gives?? I used to have to only endure the bible spewing rhetoric of the religious. Now I gotta take it from the non-believers as well? Great! You don't believe in anything. You're smarter than everyone else. Cool. What do I care? I didn't ask. And if I did, shame on me. You know who knows my true religious beliefs? Me. That's the only person who needs to know. If more people followed that rule there would be less assholes in the world.

Listen it's really admirable to have strong beliefs, whether they're strong beliefs in God, strong beliefs in Science or strong beliefs in absolutely nothing. The best part about your beliefs is that they belong to you and no one can ever take them away from you. With that said, they're YOUR beliefs and not everyone is going to agree with them nor do they have to. If people have different beliefs from you it doesn't make them wrong and you right; them dumb and you smart. To this I say, Don't Be an Asshole!

Everyone is allowed to have their own opinion about God or the complete lack thereof. Since there is no <u>irrefutable</u> evidence to prove EITHER side, guess what? NO ONE'S right. Can we just agree on that? Just don't feel the need to beat people over the head with your beliefs and expect them to change theirs. Not fair. Not cool. Complete asshole move.

Getting in between believers and non-believers is a losing proposition. Steer clear of these rivals whenever possible. The only people who are truly "in the know" are dead and they're keeping quiet.

2) **Assholes at the Movies**

This one I take very seriously as going to the movies is practically a religious experience for me. Good movies, bad movies, funny movies, scary movies...heck, even the occasional chick flick. I love 'em all. I love sitting in those mushy seats surrounded by strangers in total darkness waiting for the trailers to start. I love saving my Snow Caps for when the feature presentation begins. I love sound systems that rattle my teeth. I even love rupturing my bladder waiting for the movie to end because I don't want to miss anything by going to the bathroom. I love the whole experience. Except for one thing...assholes! And for some reason the movies are riddled with them. I think it must be the darkness. People must believe that because the lights are dim they are invisible and therefore able to do whatever stupid thing they want. Don't really know. Why spend a decent amount of money to just to go somewhere and be an asshole in the dark? Do that at home for free. Here are some good examples of what I mean...

The Late Bloomers:

The assholes that come in 20 minutes after the movie has begun and spend another 20 minutes trying to find a seat. Are they at least quiet about it? No. Do they try to duck down or look for a seat from the aisle where they're out of the way? Hell no. The REAL assholes in this group expect YOU to move so they can sit together. Here's an idea, plan better, get to the movie earlier or see a later showing. Fuck off. My wife's purse is sitting in that seat and it doesn't feel like moving.

The Baby Boomers:

No, not the generation; the people that take babies to movies made for adults. If you're taking a baby to see the newest animated adventure from Pixar, fine. No big deal. No one's gonna hear that baby crying over the 60 OTHER babies screaming anyway. Have at it. But if you're taking that baby into an R or even PG rated film, you're an asshole. When my son was little we either got a sitter for a few hours or WE DIDN'T GO. The same holds true for my daughter now. Unless the baby is a legitimate fan of Liam Neeson and enjoys watching grown men get violently slaughtered by wolves, it's probably not going to enjoy a film like *The Grey*. In fact, it's probably going to have the royal shit scared out of it, both figuratively and literally, once the scary parts jump on screen larger than life, and it's going to verbalize its dismay by screaming at the top of its lungs in a pitch that makes most people want to claw their own eardrums out. Don't be an asshole. If you don't have child care, don't go to the movies. It's really just as simple as that. You're ruining it for EVERYONE in that theater. Why do that? Going to the movies isn't a necessity. You don't HAVE to go. You go because you like it or because it's raining or because it's your third date and you're out of ideas or because you just have nothing better to do. But you do it without the presence of your etiquette impaired offspring. Even if you run out of the theater as soon as the baby starts screaming, it's too late. You've taken everyone out of the moment or made them miss something important by breaking their concentration. Seriously, if you do that...STOP DOING IT. Asshole!

Asshole Phone Home:

Ahhh, the cell phone users. We'll talk about these folks in greater detail in a later chapter but the ones I'm talking about here need no introduction. The assholes who are so oblivious to their own actions they actually partake in cell phone conversations DURING a movie. Really? I don't mean picking up a call from your neighbor who just texted to say your house is on fire. By all means ANSWER THAT! To Hell with the movie. No, I'm talking about the assholes that answer calls or make outgoing calls to just...bullshit; and in their regular voice no less. These have to be the most brazen, I-don't-give-a-fuck types of assholes in existence. If you don't know you're being an asshole by doing something like that then you have bigger problems. Hey! Asshole! If you absolutely, positively HAVE to tell your "boy" RIGHT NOW about the stupid shit you did today or the stupid shit you're planning on doing later, take it the fuck outside. No one else cares.

The Fidgeters:

Although not technically a word, I'm referring to the assholes who can't keep still for two hours. The chair kickers, the constant butt adjusters and perhaps the worst ones of all...the jimmy legs. The jimmy legs are the ones who make one or both of their legs hop up and down on the balls of their feet in rapid succession causing the entire row to vibrate. If you're that jittery, take a Xanax or muscle relaxer or something. Just stop moving for Pete's sake. What are you five??

The Stirrup Sitters:

If there's no one sitting anywhere near the space in front of you, sit any way you like. However, if there IS someone there keep your feet off their chair. I'm not your gynecologist therefore I don't care to see your foot on both sides of my peripheral vision. Unless I'm allowed to pour my soda into your Toms, move your stupid hooves. Also, there is no way to put your foot on someone's chair without them feeling it. I don't care how gently you think you're doing it. No. Way. So just sit like a big boy for now. You can do it.

The Talking Assholes:

These are the assholes that apparently think they're sitting in their living rooms at home and just taaaaalk and taaaaalk through the whole damn movie. The narrators. The "what'd he say?"-ers. The joke crackers. The incessantly talking, never shut-upping, self-important morons that are clueless to their environment. I love movie trailers. I'll go to a later showing if I'm too late for the previews but I understand that's still "buffer" time for people to get situated and finish up their conversations. Fine, but when that movie starts...shut the fuck up!

Are you comfy? Would you like a foot rub...or some $12 candy? Let me know if my back gets in the way of your feet at any time. I'm here for YOU after all!

3)   Political Assholes

As I write this, the U.S. is in the throes of my absolute LEAST favorite season...election season. This is the time when assholes from all over the country, who have been hibernating the last three and a half years suddenly awaken from their dormancy, completely pissed and thirsty for blood. They don't care whose blood either. Friends, relatives, co-workers...children; it doesn't matter the prey as long as they get their satisfaction.

This is truly a cunning species of asshole. They operate under the guise of debate but it's not debate they're after at all. They want you to engage with them but they aren't really interested in what you have to say (unless you side with them), because it's wrong, and they won't rest until you KNOW it's wrong, or give up. You don't have a difference of opinion; you have a mental disability that doesn't allow you to think like them. What other explanation could there be after all? Why else would you be so stupid? Maybe it's because the media has brainwashed you...or maybe it's because you're ignorant and can't think for yourself. That's gotta be it.

To get into a conversation with a political asshole about politics is akin to breaking down a brick wall with your forehead. You're never going to get through and you will be left with a horrific headache. The best is to avoid the topic with anyone and everyone unless 1) they share your views or 2) you feel like getting into an argument. If you sincerely think you're changing anyone's mind you've either lost yours or you really ARE ignorant.

Most people know the basic unwritten rules of engagement when it comes to this topic and stay as far away from it as possible. If they do bring it up they'll test the waters first with something simple and if the response comes back different from what they had hoped, they let it go. Others are different. Others enjoy bathing in the contempt they have for the "other side"; the losers, the idiots, the morally corrupt. They have so much pent up anger and hatred towards their supposed fellow man and they don't care who gets caught in the crossfire. I'm not saying don't support your candidate of choice with a yard sign or bumper sticker or by "liking" them on Facebook but just understand that because this country is so polarized, you've just alienated 50% of the population. Half the people around you now have a beef with you. A lot of you are thinking "Who cares?? I'll say or do what I want and they can all go to Hell if they don't like it". That's a completely healthy and legitimate position and that works for most people. I, on the other hand, would rather just save myself the aggravation. For one, I've never driven through a neighborhood and seen a political yard sign and thought "Man, those people have really nice hedges and they're for the other guy. I'm gonna vote for the other guy now. Anyone with hedges like that can't be wrong." I've also never done that after seeing a bumper sticker on a car. You know what I secretly but always do when I see a sign or sticker? I either think to myself "hey look, another smart person like me" if they're promoting my candidate, or "What an idiot. What's wrong with that person, seriously?" if they're promoting the other candidate. The best thing you can do is keep it to yourself and go vote for who you want when the day comes and then go on with your life. It's not about being cowardly, it's about being civilized.

I see people every day on Facebook blasting supporters of "the other side" for being so stupid. They call names and point fingers and basically insult the crap out of anyone unfortunate enough to read their meaningless rant. What's the point? To piss off half of your friends and family? Post topics and legitimate discussions but don't resort to name calling and idea bashing. Just be cool. Those 3 words may sound silly and cliché but that could be one of the most powerful statements in the English language. I wish more people heeded its message.

Inspiration Intermission #1

Hey look, you made it. I'm proud of you! Now put the knife down and drench your senses in the positivity of the next few paragraphs.

The Diamond in the Rough.

A New York City woman was recently enjoying a leisurely day at the park with her 2 year old twins. Prior to placing her daughter into one of the swings, she removed her ring, applied sunscreen to the toddler and placed the ring on the stroller.

Two days later on her way to work she realized she wasn't wearing it so she headed back to her apartment to find it. Then she remembered... (insert dramatic music). She searched the stroller to no avail.

Little did she know, an attorney and fellow mom had found her ring in the grass at the park. For two days she placed flyers in the neighborhood, left a note at the park, placed online ads and even one in the Lost and Found section of Craig's List. She was about to give up hope and give the ring to the police when lo and behold she received an email from the rightful owner of the ring who had seen the posting on Craig's List.

The two made arrangements over the phone to meet and make the transfer. As an expression of gratitude the mom presented the attorney with a gift card to enjoy a night on the town and as a sincere Thank You for being honest.

See? Doesn't that feel good? Now back to the assholes...

4)   Auto Assholes

Assholes on the road. This one has the potential to fill a whole book. Because of the sheer numbers involved I'm sure I won't even scratch the surface when it comes to this topic so just bear with me.

Who hasn't experienced assholes while driving? Show of hands. Anyone? I didn't think so. This is a topic everyone holds near and dear to their hearts, or at least the darkest part of their hearts. You can find every type of asshole I listed before cluttering up the roadways and perhaps that is why this list can be so long. Let's get right to it, shall we?

The Perpetually Blinking Asshole:

This is the asshole that has their turn signal on for 17 miles at a time causing people to either A) slow down to give them room to move over or B) speed up so as not to allow them the option (another asshole). I hear this can be an easy mistake to make but I'm rapidly approaching 40 years old now and I still haven't done this myself. The cool thing about turn signals or "blinkers" is that not only do they flash on and off on the OUTSIDE of the vehicle but also on the INSIDE. This alerts the driver that said blinker is turned on. The flashing light is also accompanied by an annoying clicking sound for the same purpose. Do these people just never look down at their instrument panels? Is the radio too loud? Are they too busy texting, eating, applying makeup or smoking a joint to notice? I try to entertain myself by waiting until they actually DO need to get over and seeing if they finally notice, but it's not really that entertaining either way. It's more fun to drive next to them and try to use hand gestures to let them know their turn signal is on. The problem is the only gesture I can ever think of looks like I'm trying to squeeze their boob. If you're ever driving and some dude is next to you making boob-squeezing motions with his hand, it's probably me and I'm either looking to get to second base or tell you that your turn signal is on. *However, if you allow the boob squeeze I will forget about the annoying turn signal.

*Man boobs do not qualify.

Give Me a Sign, Asshole:

This is the complete opposite of the Perpetually Blinking Asshole. This asshole NEVER uses a turn signal. Moving an arm 5 inches and pushing that little steering wheel appendage up or down a notch is just far too much trouble. The people behind them will know they're turning soon enough, if they don't rear end them first. I'm not psychic and I don't know if I'll ever be (because again, I'm not psychic) so you need to let me know if you're turning or scooting on over into my lane. I know it's a pain in the ass to move that much but we'd all appreciate it.

Stop...Asshole Time!:

These are the assholes that hit their brake every 4 seconds for reasons completely unknown to everyone but themselves. There are no cars in front of them; they're not speeding; there are no traffic lights; yet they're braking constantly. Are they hallucinating? Do they see cute little bunnies running across the road? What gives? You know what also slows down a moving car? Letting up on the gas. You don't have to brake unless you're trying to stop, yield, slow down or be an asshole.

Life in the Fast Lane:

These assholes will surely make you lose your mind. Most highways or interstates are configured with two driving types in mind; fast drivers and slow drivers. It is common knowledge (or should be) that the left lane is for those going the speed limit and over. The right lane is typically for those going the speed limit and under. There are even posted signs that say "Slower Traffic Keep Right". The speeders didn't put those up, the government did. Why? So people who aren't comfortable going fast in their cars know to stay in the right lane and this eases traffic and promotes a congestion-free commuting experience. Simple right? Apparently not so much, or at least not for assholes. No, these pricks are happy to drive 300 miles doing 45 in a 70 all the way. They'll hold up traffic for miles if they have to. They're impervious to flashing high beams, horn honking, waving fists, tailgating, mooning, throwing loose change...everything. They're not getting over.

If you can't notice you're going slower than everyone else and there's a line of angry drivers behind you, you're either just not paying attention or you're purposely being an asshole. I tend to believe the latter. Only because I know people who have admitted during conversations with me on this very topic that say "To hell with those people. They can go around me if they don't like it". So they're doing it on purpose. Why? A control issue maybe, or a problem with authority. I'm not really sure. Personally I would much rather move over, even if I'm speeding myself, than to have a more aggressive driver hugging my rear bumper. It's not a sign of weakness people, it's just being courteous. Plus you always have the possibility of seeing a speeder get pulled over after letting him or her pass which can be one of the most gratifying events one can witness.

The Smoking Asshole:

Having been a smoker myself for many years I'm not going to get on my high horse now and pretend I'm better than that. I honestly just loved the title "smoking asshole". It brings such funny imagery to my mind. Try it, I'll wait..............See? I just pictured an ass with a monocle, a top hat, a handlebar moustache and a cigarette on one of those old-timey, long cigarette holders sticking out of the hole. That's fucking hilarious.

OK, well I guess since I listed it though I need to have some kind of beef to go on about. Let's see. Well, I guess a few things come to mind. If you smoke and the others in the car don't, don't light up anyway, even if it's your car. That's just being an asshole. Also, I know most cars don't come with an ashtray which leads a lot of smokers to just flick their butts out the window. There are a few problems associated with that. One, it litters the world with disgusting cigarette butts and that makes Indians cry (http://www.youtube.com/watch?v=j7OHG7tHrNM) and nobody wants that. Haven't they been through enough? Two, when you're driving down the road and flicking your butt out, the wind can carry it and deliver it straight to the person's windshield behind you. This can be exceptionally frightening at night as the embers explode in the unsuspecting driver's face like their own private-yet-unwelcomed fireworks display. Three, it's a fire hazard. It's fine if you need your nicotine fix just try not to take out 500 acres of protected woodlands in the process. I'm pretty sure that would make Indians cry as well. Just keep an empty soda can or bottle in the car and throw it in there. Easy peasy lemon squeezy.

The Ass on your Ass:

These are the assholes that find it necessary to drive inches away from the back of your vehicle. The tailgaters. If you're going too slow (by which I define as slower than the posted speed limit for no real reason) then it's your own fault...BUT if you're moving right along there's no reason for this. A good combatant to the *Ass on your Asses* are the *Stop...Asshole Timers*. Nothing makes the tailgaters back off like a few good, sudden and unpredicted taps on the brakes.

How Do You Spell Asshole?:

The texters. Texting and driving. Need I really say more? So much attention has been brought to this topic that there's not much else I can add. If what you're doing can kill someone, you're practicing asshole behavior. Don't do it.

Calling all Assholes:

Talking on the phone is easy. Driving is easy. Then why do so many people have such a hard time doing both simultaneously? You're just TALKING, asshole! You don't need to mentally transport yourself to another dimension as you envision every word you're hearing into a virtual reality. Just stay in the moment, remain aware of your surroundings and just talk. Seems easy enough but you see so many people driving fine and then they get a phone call and all Hell breaks loose. They start veering off the road, braking for no reason, going extra slow and forgetting where they're going or even where they're at. How do these people cope when they have passengers in the car talking to them? I'll tell ya how. These are usually the types who feel like they have to look at the person they're talking to the whole time even when they're driving. Sound travels in waves directly to my ear canals. You don't need to look at me...just drive. If you want to drive home a point just use inflection in your voice and I'll know just the same. Trust me.

Halt, You Asshole!:

The assholes that run red lights and stop signs. I don't mean yellow lights (guilty), or even yellow lights that turn red halfway through the intersection (guilty), I'm talking about "the light's been red for a few seconds, get ready to die", red lights. It's not just an asshole thing to do; it's dangerous as all get-out. Recently there was a story on my local news about how certain intersections around town had been fitted with cameras that capture the license plates of cars that run through red lights and sends them a traffic citation automatically. The reporter was interviewing person after person and they were complaining about how "it's not fair" and how their rights were somehow being trampled on. You know what's not fair? Getting T-boned by some toothless moron in a hurry to get to the liquor store. I don't wanna be

45

some sad story on the 6 o'clock news because you're out of Boone's Farm.

You Can Put Lipstick on an Asshole…:

This one goes out to the ladies (and maybe some dudes). Ladies, I love you all and I'm appreciative every day of the fact that you're the ones that give birth because otherwise the human race would have gone extinct long ago, but please, pretty please with sugar on top, DON'T put your makeup on while driving. Do it before you leave or in the parking lot of wherever it is you're going. If you really HAVE to, only do it during red lights. I know you think you're doing both well but really you're not. Not at all. You're scaring the living shit out of the rest of us but good! NO ONE can apply makeup to their freaking EYES and drive a car at the same time. At least not well. You SEE out of your eyes yet you're DRAWING on your eyes while driving. Do you see the potential problem here? Unless you have eyes that move independently from each other like a chameleon or a fish, your focus is most likely gonna be in that mirror, which makes us all screwed. Not to mention, do you realize how close you are to being called "Patchy" or "Lady Bluebeard" the rest of your life if you get in a wreck whilst pointing a PENCIL at your EYE? Just revel in the knowledge that you already possess the one part of human anatomy that makes every heterosexual male on earth your biggest fan by default. We don't really care about makeup, we love you no matter what. We'd rather just live to see our destination.

Drunk Asshole:

See "**How Do You Spell Asshole**". If you're still driving drunk you simply cannot be taught.

The Honky Asshole

Whoa! What?! Not the racial slur from the 70's, I'm talking about the assholes who have turned the sound of their car horns into a new fucking language because they use it so much. Unless you drive a cab in New York, are signaling for a drawbridge to open or summoning an army in Middle-earth lay off the God damned horn. If the light turned green 2 milliseconds ago, I don't need a hundred decibel inspiration to move. Give me a fucking moment to react. I'm texting up here! (smirk) Conversely, if the light turns green and it's been a while, you deserve a good honking.

The Deep Voiced Asshole:

Drop that bass! No, really, drop it. Stop doing it. I thought that died out in the 90's anyway. We're all very impressed that you saved up all your money from selling weed and purchased a $12,000 sound system for your Honda Civic. That was clearly a good call, no doubt. However, when I can hear you approaching from the next county there is a problem. It's like the scene from Jurassic Park when the T-Rex is walking up and the water starts rippling. There are few things more unsettling after a hard day at work than driving home through an hour and a half of bumper to bumper traffic with an asshole next to you all the way who is kind enough to share his music with all the land. Thank you kind stranger! I didn't care to hear the music (or silence) from my own car. I'd MUCH rather hear yours. Do I owe you anything? No, no, I must insist.

It really is an impressive display of sound; don't get me wrong, it just creeps me out to have my balls vibrating with my kids in the car.

All Aboard the Asshole Express:

This is just a quick little one I had to throw in. I don't know what it's like where you live but here in crazy-ville the locals have recently adopted the use of train horns in their cars and trucks. Why, you may ask? Just to be assholes really. There can be no other explanation. It works too! Whenever I nearly shit myself in traffic after Jethro in the Ford F850 next to me lays on the old train horn I think to myself, "Wow! That guy's an enormous asshole!" If you haven't heard one just go to your nearest train tracks and wait for a train. That unbearable sound you hear is coming from 140 psi's of compressed air being force fed from an air reservoir, causing a diaphragm to vibrate against a nozzle inside the horn's power chamber. It serves an important purpose when used accordingly. "Hey, look out! There's a fucking train coming!!!" It's loud because it needs to be; and when it's accompanied by A TRAIN, you're expecting it. You're not expecting it on the interstate when you're taking your first sip of coffee on your way to work. Funny? Ok, yes. I gotta admit that's funny as Hell... but it's not funny when it happens to you, so to this I say ASSHOLE!

Semi-Assholes:

Let me start out by saying I have a lot of respect for the fine men and women who drive tractor trailers for a living. Without them the world as we know it would come to a screeching halt. That said, some of them drive like the demonic semis from the 80's Stephen King movie *Maximum Overdrive*. Are they trying to deliver pallets of Ol' Roy to Wal-Mart or carve a path of death and destruction across the U.S.? When people do the asshole things I'm listing in cars it's bad enough, but when it's done in an 18 wheeled, 40 ton behemoth, whooooaa. Things like weaving in and out of traffic, tailgating and going 90 in the pouring rain. Then you get the jokers who like to play asshole games like when they drive right next to another semi and go the same slow speed, clogging up traffic for miles. Another favorite of mine is when they cut you off so they can pass a car in front of them, even though there's no one behind YOU for miles and then perform the world's slowest passing maneuver in history. Always makes me smile.

The One Armed Bandit/The Sanford and Son Asshole:

This one's a two-fer. The One Armed Bandit is the guy who transports a king sized mattress on the top of his Corolla but not to worry, he's holding it down with a bungee cord and his freaking HAND. Ya, that'll hold it down, Superman. It's no big deal until you hit a mattress that's fallen onto the road going 70...on the highway...at night...like I have. This brings me to another question. Who drops their bed and leaves it there?? If you're dumping it I understand (that's an asshole thing as well but I get it), but transporting it? Didn't you need it? Anyway, back to topic...I understand if you don't have a truck or can't afford to spring for delivery but you're not fooling anyone with that arm trick. You just look like an asshole.

The other asshole I'm including in this section is the guy who piles 4000 pounds of crap in the bed of the smallest truck he could find and stacks it in a way that resembles an almost finished game of Jenga. Again, bungee cords are used. Bungee cords with the tensile strength well below what they're attempting to hold but they're there for moral support if nothing else. Let's see, you got a water heater on top of a rusted washing machine on top of a broken treadmill...better throw a second bungee on there just to be safe.

The Lost Asshole:

This particular asshole actually seems to have special powers and is not to be trifled with. He can singlehandedly irritate everyone else on the road with an array of idiotic maneuvers, fake outs and moronic stunt work. The lost assholes greatest hits include, but are absolutely not limited to: Turning suddenly without signaling, almost always at the last possible second leaving the car behind to execute a physics defying shimmy to avoid collision. Signaling but never actually turning, leaving his fellow drivers to clench their steering wheels, in a patience draining heightened state of anticipation. And, of course, the piece de resistance, the masterstroke if you will, of slowing down suddenly and dramatically neither signaling nor turning but instead just...looking...deciding...debating...

Completely and utterly dumbfounded right there in the middle of the road, carelessly leading his fellow travelers in a rousing game of pin the front bumper on the asshole.

Not only can the lost asshole irritate every other vehicle unfortunate enough to share the road with them, they can turn the person in the passenger seat into an absolute asshole by association. Often times the lost asshole's passenger will incite just as much anger amongst other drivers as the asshole himself. They are not driving but something about them will ensure that onlookers dislike them. It could be their hair, their flying hand gestures, ridiculous nodding in agreement with the lost asshole, their face, something about them is guaranteed to be offensive to angry motorists – it is the curse of travelling with the lost asshole.

The Slow Turner:

Those glorious individuals that feel the need to come to a complete stop before making a turn in front of you; nearly causing a 12 car pileup. What is the reason here? No power steering? Are they transporting a pyramid of champagne glasses? I'm not saying you need to power slide into your destination like a stunt car driver but c'mon people! There's a certain traffic tempo we're all used to and when you're off-beat like that it screws up the entire congested concerto.

The 4 Way Asshole:

I love the 4 way asshole. They are competitive, spirited, unreasonable and unpredictable. The 4 way asshole is the true gamer of the road. This asshole challenges you to a game you will never win. It is a match of endurance, hair trigger reflexes, ignorance and a complete lack of common sense. All the elements to make any game interesting are present when the 4 way asshole is in the mix. At a 4 way stop is where the game begins and ends. It is a one round match with the odds stacked heavily in the favor of the asshole. This is the stronghold of the 4 way asshole, this is where his assholeyness truly blossoms and he is indeed king.

The average driver stands little chance of winning. When you arrive into the arena of the asshole, the rules of the road and general courtesy vanish. In their place the rules of the asshole reign supreme. You know the scenario. You both arrive at the intersection at the same time because it is the assholes lucky day. He lives for these moments of serendipity. You look at each other. You, being a rational person, assess the situation. He, being the 4 way asshole however, does not. He looks you in the eye, nods at you. You take this as a sign that it is your move. You start to move forward with some confidence, but lo and behold Mr. Asshole moves at the same time as you. He has tricked you and your confidence turns to concern. He looks at you again. You look at him. You signal him to go first, in a meek attempt to preserve your own safety but he insists no-no-no, you may pass first and he waves you through. You start to move forward again, and strike you down with a feather, the asshole also moves forward. Your eyes lock for the third time. This time Mr. Asshole shakes his fist at your moronic behavior, flips you the bird, screeches his tires as he zooms through the intersection shaking his head and obviously muttering words about your intelligence and possibly even your virtue. And there you sit. Dumbfounded. Like a kicked puppy. You have lost the game at the 4 way intersection. The asshole is still king. Assholes of the intersection, there are hardly words for your driving prowess.

The other game they like to play is a fascinating societal folly called "How important am I?" The goal is to prove your importance by waiting for no one. It doesn't matter if you're the last one to arrive at the intersection, you're going FIRST! Why? Because God Dammit you're more important and you don't have to wait for anyone or anything! Suck on it losers! SCREEEEEEEEEEEEEEECH....

5)   Parking Lot Assholes

The Double Wide Asshole:

Oh asshole of the double wide variety you are the nightmare of the parking lot. These poor chaps suffer from a particularly tragic form of the asshole disorder. It leaves them unable to deal appropriately with space, clear guidelines, basic geometry, and general courtesy. Double wide assholes render non-assholes everywhere helpless and furious. This asshole is diagnosed by the symptom of being able to take up two parking spaces at the same time, more often than not with a very small car. A true gift indeed. This confounding ability is also more often than not put to use during the times when parking spaces are in their highest demand and you are already feeling a little anxious and homicidal. This is where the double wide asshole is right at home. Thank you assholes, thank you!

Example #1 – Nailed it!

Example #2 – This was in a crowded hospital garage.
(Lines highlighted to show position)
Bravo, asshole!

The "You Snooze, You Lose" Asshole:

The snooze you lose asshole loves to alert you to the fact that you are too slow. They much prefer to show you rather than tell you, and a parking space stealing demonstration is just what this asshole thinks you need. Your space is where this asshole finds his place in the delicate parking lot ecosystem. You have probably met one, and you probably didn't enjoy the experience. This is the parking lot sniper, the good mood assassin and the downright dirty space-stealing asshole. This specimen comes out of the woodwork right about the time you are signaling to claim your spot, he sweeps in like the reaper and you find yourself a homeless victim of the snooze you lose asshole. Your spot becomes his spot and you're generally not quite sure what just happened. Was he there all along and I just didn't see him? Did I black out? Is it ME who's the asshole? You have been sniped, plain and simple. You have suffered an injustice and apart from piss and moan there is little you can do that keeps you within the confines of our pesky assault and battery laws. The snooze you lose asshole flirts with danger, but sleeps well in the knowledge that you can do nothing about their existence without becoming the very thing you despise most...an asshole.

The Close Parker:

The close parking asshole is the evil genius of this group as a whole. They use their asshole superpowers to force you into a routine of slapstick comedy. There is a good chance these assholes hang around to see the result of their work. Why buy the ticket if you are not going to stay for the show right? So there you are, having survived the treacherous ordeal of actually getting a spot in the first place and surviving the barbarian hordes at Wal-Mart. Then, just as you are strolling back to your space with the true victory of a successful journey in your grasp, you see your car. And then you see another car. And if you look closely you can make out an ever-so-slight presence of sunlight between your car and the other car. The close parker likes to snuggle right in close to the driver's side, and finds a joy in the fact that there is no way you can get into your seat using the traditional method. Chances are that around this time, you start a little asshole tirade in your head, or under your breath, or, if the close parker really hits the jackpot you start to very audibly verbalize the situation. This is where the close parking asshole gets to reap the rewards of his labor. There is probably nothing quite as satisfying as seeing you enter your car from the passenger's seat, and shimmy over to the driver's seat. With a little bit of good grace from the gods, the close parker snickering in the distance may even get to see you hit your head, or have a brief and unexpected (and possibly enjoyable?) encounter with the handbrake. The close parker is the purest blend of comedian and ass. They should be commended for their dedication to asshole mastery.

This was submitted by my cousin. His car is the one on the right. Notice the complete absence of any other vehicles around anywhere. This guy was a pro!

Being an Asshole is not a Handicap:

Assholes in the handicap spots. It is hard not to like these ones. We can all appreciate that these assholes recognize that they do have a terrible disability and admitting that one has a problem is indeed the first step on the road to recovery. However, assholes, there are more needy people than you, and they deserve these spots more than you do. There is an entire parking lot for you to terrorize, so go forth and prosper in the parking arena! Are you such an asshole that you think people that can't WALK don't need to be closer to the door? Or are you so kind that you realize you should not be allowed amongst the democratic parking system where the innocent are at your mercy? Either way, unless you are disabled both by your asshole disorder and have need for a wheelchair, you do not belong in these parking spaces so stop using them. You will be a better asshole for it. OH! And one more thing, you're not fooling anyone with that handicap tag you "borrowed" from your bed ridden grandmother. We can all see you hop out of the car just fine. It doesn't make it ok because you have a tag; it just makes you an even bigger asshole.

The Hauling Ass-Hole:

The assholes that speed in parking lots. This is the adrenalin junkie of the asshole family. The hauling asshole seems to think that hurtling along in confined spaces at the speed of sound is a great idea. No matter the blind corners and tight turns, this is the world of the hauling asshole, where putting men, women, children, the elderly and the handicapped in danger is so very okay. The more obstacles there are, the more riveting the spectacle of inappropriate velocity and impending doom for some unsuspecting innocent. Everything is fair game when Mr. Hauling Hole is around. This asshole gathers his joy by setting a break-neck pace at half second intervals. The stop-start show put on by the hauling asshole is a satisfying blend of sudden braking, screeching tires, near misses and complete disregard for public safety. Danger is the name of the game here. Hey asshole, thanks so much for including us in your little death lottery. We really appreciate it.

The Middle of the Road Asshole:

Here we have our daredevil assholes. The middle of the road asshole has absolutely no problem risking life and limb for a casual stroll across the road. No, not ACROSS the road...make that IN the road. They are either too self-important or too stupid to move out of the way of moving cars. Not only do they walk in the middle of the road, but they do it as slowly as they can. To make matters worse, they'll look right at you and give YOU dirty looks for getting too close, almost TAUNTING you to hit them. How about this, asshole, get the fuck out of the way! Near misses and bewildered drivers abound in the presence of the middle of the road asshole. These fascinating mouth breathers are more than happy to wander through traffic on foot with no obvious rush or concern for their own safety. You have the car but make no mistake; this asshole is in the driver's seat. Those controlling a vehicle are in a lose-lose situation here, and oh boy does the middle of the road asshole know it. If you are unlucky enough to actually hit one, you are a villain (although it might feel really good for just a sec). You are a reckless driver who has failed at all the basics of driving; failing to swerve, failing to brake, failing to pay attention, failing at life really – yep. You're an asshole. And in a true disservice to justice, any miraculous maneuver that you do pull out of the bag to preserve this particular asshole's life is never hailed as anything but expected. Of course you should have braked, swerved and given yourself whiplash. THERE WAS A PERSON IN THE MIDDLE OF THE ROAD! Ahhh, this is a treacherous form of asshole to be sure. The middle of the road asshole wins, even if he dies. Son of a .....

Close parkers suck at parallel parking too!

Geez. This is getting heavy. Let's take a breather with this feel good story.

Every Bunny's Free to Feel Good.

A mom and her adorable 3 year old daughter were recently exiting a train in a bustling northeastern city. The little girl was in her stroller and accompanied by her dearest friend, her stuffed bunny. All was well in the world until the bunny decided to make a run for it and plummeted onto the train tracks below.

Now, being the father of a 4 year old girl myself, I more than understand the immense seriousness of a situation like this. My daughter has a stuffed bear she calls "B" that she has had almost since birth. She cannot, WILL not, go ANYWHERE without this bear. At this point it is a bear by name only. What it more closely resembles is a dreadlocked mass of road kill. Washing it has only made its appearance more grotesque and has really done nothing about its smell which is one I will spare you the details on. No I won't. It smells like a mix of stale vomit, a well-used gymnasium and the souls of a thousand rancid juice boxes. I don't know how she even likes having this thing in her vicinity, let alone in her constant embrace. It got so bad that I found a model number on it and found the exact same bear on eBay which I promptly ordered. My excitement was palpable. You would have thought the bear was for ME. In a way I guess it was. Much to my dismay, "New B" was discarded as the cheap imposter he was and exiled to the bowels of the toy chest along with all the other second fiddles. I gotta commend her on her loyalty though.

Whenever my wife and I cannot locate "B" we both have mild to serious panic attacks depending on how long B is missing. The thought of losing it has actually given us nightmares. Thankfully he's always shown up somewhere. Anyway, back to our story…

So here they sat, a mom and her daughter shocked and dumbfounded as the little girls nearest and dearest friend lay there, out of reach and in the path of an oncoming train. The mother tried to remedy the situation by explaining how they'd get a new one. Ya, good luck with that. That wasn't gonna fix anything. There was going to be some therapy in both of their futures for sure.

What they didn't know was that some transit authority workers had witnessed the horrifying event and were busy setting the wheels in motion for a death-defying rescue. One worker called the dispatcher and they were able to halt the oncoming train in time for the other workers to remove the bunny from its perilous predicament and save the day. They returned the bunny to the waiting arms of its rightful owner and all was right with the world again.

I think it's pretty cool that transit workers took time out of their day to save a little girl's stuffed rabbit. They could have ignored the situation and done nothing. Who cares?

It's just a stuffed rabbit, right? Instead they went out of their way to be helpful. Assholes? Not on THEIR watch!

Refreshing eh? Well don't get too comfortable.

More assholes on the way.

6) Assholes in the Sky

Assholes in the sky are a different breed of asshole. And if I may, rather than just identify the varieties and traits of these assholes, I would also like to incorporate advice on how to deal with them. This is my little contribution to safety in the sky.

Management Plan:

When an asshole gets a bit of air, he or she can really come into their own. Being seated next to a flying asshole is not only a woeful stroke of terrible luck but it also comes with a whole host of responsibilities. You didn't deserve it. It is not your fault. But this is how assholes work. On the flight, it is your job to minimize the asshole whenever possible, to never provoke an adverse asshole reaction – you owe this to your fellow travelers, and to appropriately engage and disengage with the asshole as necessary. The flying asshole has a myriad of habits. The first sign that the asshole beside you is starting to flex, is the constant need to attend to whatever prize is stashed in the overhead locker. Standing up frequently to rummage overhead is a sure sign you are on board with an asshole. If you are lucky, said asshole will reach overhead and in doing so, simultaneously give you a glimpse of either belly or ass crack, depending on which side you are seated and of course assault you with the heavy breathing and snorting associated with the effort. Assholes have terrible cardio fitness. It is just a fact. Sitting directly across the aisle from one of these is really the shortest of straws. You get the asshole right in the face for as long as he is tending to business overhead.

Sign two of the flying asshole is the food issue. Assholes like food. They like to get it. They like to eat it. They like to complain about it. Then they like to talk about it. A lot. If the asshole is in peak condition you will be asked if you want your food, if you are going to eat the rest of your food, and if you agree that the food is indeed terrible. An asshole does like to be agreed with. A word of warning, never agree. But never disagree. A shoulder shrug is the best option. Conversing with an airborne asshole is never what you want to do. They are not really talking to you; they are trying to enlist you as a co-asshole so be very careful.

As the flight progresses you will come face to face with an asshole and its bathroom needs. For non assholes a trip to the bathroom is not a big deal. But for an asshole it is an assy opportunity. They are most likely to time their run to coincide with the time the aisle is blocked by the flight attendants and their trusty cart. The cart fills the space where the asshole needs to be and the issue becomes a full blown encounter. When an asshole can't pass, there becomes a problem. The asshole has a couple of options. He can huff and puff and demand they move because he is having an asshole emergency. Or he can go back to his seat and wait. This is not the option you want them to take. The risk is very high that the asshole will come back and talk to you about his asshole problem. You will have a very long flight, and your shoulders will ache from the near constant shrugging. If it gets too much, you should progress to perhaps head nodding, head shaking, and if you are really in trouble you could incorporate the eye roll.

Flying assholes get sick. They do it to be assholes. And they do it on full flights where there is nowhere else to sit but beside you. First class is full, the medical seats are full, and the flight attendants aren't paid enough to seat a sick asshole too close to their seats. They may be sick because of the aforementioned food, or because of the aforementioned aisle blocking maneuver perpetrated by the attendants. Either way, you may be stuck next to a sick asshole who is coughing, spluttering, rumbling or if you have the ultimate luck, they may be regurgitating into a little paper bag. If this happens, you have mismanaged your asshole responsibilities and are in fact being punished by cosmic asshole justice. I can think of no other explanation, and cannot help you any further. I can only encourage you to think about where you went wrong, and learn from your mistakes.

In the interest of time and space I will list out several varieties of asshole commonly found on airplanes and not mentioned before. I won't go into detail on each one as I believe they are self-explanatory and one could write forever on this topic. Here we go:

The Chair Kicker
The Whistler
The Back of Your Chair Leaner
The Hummer
The Chair Hogger
The Singer

The Armrest Hogger
The Fidgeter
The Middle Seat Fully Opened Newspaper Reader
The Leg Kicker
The Sloppy Sleeper
The Chronic Bathroom Breaker
The Snorer
The Constant Window Opener/Closer
The Panic Attacker
The Overhead Light Lover
The Constant Griper
The Alcoholic
The Chatty Kathy
The Smelly Food Eater
The Farter
The Deodorant Hater
The Shoe Remover
The Loud Talker
And everyone's favorite...

The Screaming Child
(but only if the parents aren't even TRYING to control him/her)

7)   Pedestrian Assholes

The Life is a Highway Asshole:

The life is a highway asshole, blazes his own trail. Never mind the ones actually set aside for walkers and runners. No way man! There are roads for vehicles and there are paths for people but there are no boundaries that can contain the life is a highway asshole. These foot soldiers pose an interesting situation to citizens like you and me. They taunt you with their fitness prowess and how they have managed to get off their assholes and run, walk or jog their way to a life that is better than yours. They blind you with their neon "I am an athlete" outfits, from their multi colored Nike shoes, to the reflective flak jacket they feel the need to wear in broad daylight, these assholes are superior to you and your beer belly and you will damn well respect them. Not only do they throw their superior assholes in your face, they lurk where people are not supposed to lurk. They tread upon grass that is not meant to be trodden on; they spring from behind clouds, trees and phone booths like supernatural beings, to show you that they will not use the paths that tax payers provide, no. Hell no! The bumpy, street pavement is WAY more fun to walk or run on than that nice smooth sidewalk that stretches for miles in every direction and lies a safe distance from life-ending road ragers. Plus the added adrenaline from all the close calls really gets their heart racing for a more intense cardio fitness routine. Lead, follow or get out of the way, bitches!

The Steel Curtain Asshole:

The steel curtain asshole relies on a team of supporting assholes. Generally, there will be a ringleader of the group and it is their collective mission, nay, their pleasure to create a moving wall of assholes. They are organized, menacing and skilled in the art of seeming oblivious. This squad will block the sidewalk, the path or the general direction in which you are trying to move, with frightening telepathic skill and a natural ease. On the sidewalk they will dawdle, browse, stop without warning and shuffle from left to right to stop you from penetrating their asshole wall. They know all your moves, they are ahead of your game and you absolutely will not bust through until they allow it. When they are done toying with you, they will step aside in unison, and watch you stomp by while you contain all your fury over the game that has just been played with you. The steel curtain asshole revels in the mastery of their talents and there is nothing you can do about them. This is their world, we just live in it.

Inspiration Intermission #3

So is everyone an asshole? Not at all, check this out:

Tipping is Not a City in China

A couple dines at an Italian restaurant in Houston, TX. Their bill comes and it's $27. They leave the waiter an 18,518% tip. Now THAT'S a good tipper!

The couple, who were regulars at the restaurant, found out that their waiter had recently lost his vehicle in a severe storm and was having to use the public transit system to get to and from work. The couple was very fond of the waiter since he had always provided exceptional service and felt he deserved some help so they took it upon themselves to intervene. They handed the waiter an envelope with FIVE THOUSAND DOLLARS CASH in it to help him buy a new car. That must have been some outstanding service! I'm talking johnny-on-the-spot with the refills, multiple breadstick baskets and all the parmesan cheese you can stomach kind of service; and even THEN I'm quite positive I wouldn't give someone 5 grand. In fact I'm 18,518% positive I wouldn't!

The waiter was completely overwhelmed to say the least. He immediately hopped a bus to Reno and bet it all on red. Noooo, not really. He put it towards a new set of wheels.

Nice...that was nice. Now where were we?

Ooooh, riiiight...

8)   Assholes at Home

Knock Knock Assholes:

Saying No –

Knock-knock. Who's there? It's probably an asshole. These door knockers are a strange breed of asshole. They can flip your day upside down just by the very act of showing up on your doorstep. They are a punch line in a bad joke, and they seem to know it too. But this doesn't stop them knocking on your door with offerings of everything from vacuum cleaners to steak. These are an amazing group of assholes with the gift of disbelief and bewilderment. They have bothered to knock on your door, offering you the bargain of a lifetime and you have the audacity to say no! To deny them their living, to insult their profession! You brute, you heartless soul-crusher, you all around bad person. These assholes turn the tables on you, on your very own doorstep. When they knock on your door, they are the asshole, but as soon as you say no thank you, you become the asshole. It is both tragic and magic what these assholes do to you with a simple knock-knock. Well done asshole, well done.

Saying Yes -

Knock-knock. Hello Asshole. Yes! I would love to purchase that set of steak knives from you. When this happens, the asshole is encouraged. Now, encouraging assholes is ill advised, dangerous and very unfair to the rest of your fellow man. All it takes is one simple yes and the asshole gets reward and validation, the asshole seems to double in size with this boost in confidence. The tables will turn on you if you fall for this. You will get repeat assholes, friends of the asshole, and someday the asshole will show up with a one legged rabbit that is cute as hell, and a small child with a disability and ask you if you would like to buy a poisonous spider. You will only have yourself to blame. Encouraging knock-knock assholes only results in more knock-knocking.

Ringing Assholes:

When assholes are given a telephone the entire world is at risk. An asshole can get to anyone with a phone. These inappropriate assholes call your home at all hours of the day. They call with amazing offers, from wireless connections to coat hangers; boy do these assholes have something for you. Some of them are even kind enough to call you from foreign parts of the globe. I don't know about you, but the offer of having my computer checked for viruses by a prestigious company in Bangladesh sounds like a great idea! If by great idea, we mean absolutely moronic. If you have become an assholes greatest dream and actually agree to a service like this, perhaps you could also ask for a deal on getting your prostate checked at the same time. It makes sense since you are bending over anyway.

The Mrs. Kravitz Asshole:

If you're unfamiliar with the name Mrs. Kravitz, it's the name of the nosey, busybody neighbor on the old TV show Bewitched. I recommend catching some old episodes on TV or YouTube if you've never experienced it. To see her is to truly loathe her. The asshole next door sadly is not a fleeting asshole. This is not an asshole that will only destroy your day the one time. This is a chronic asshole. The most trying of them all, because they are the most dedicated. These assholes don't rely on the asshole gift alone. These assholes train, and rehearse and plan. They are the Olympians of assholes. Often they are older than you and they don't have a job. They have nothing but time. Time to craft strategies designed especially for you. Tailored perfectly to suit all they know about what really pisses you off. They will do whatever it takes to know what you are doing and then attack you with the perfect plan to have you rue the day you were ever born. They know what time you like to wake up in the weekends, so naturally, they will time a good bit of lawn mowing about two hours before you are ready to wake up on a Sunday morning. They can turn a simple walk to the mailbox into the Spanish Inquisition. They want to know every detail about your personal life and are not afraid to ask you straight-out. If you're talking to friends outside they will magically appear and start sweeping pavement that's already swept and watering plants that have already been watered just to try and covertly gather personal information on the sly. Only they're not sly. They're painfully obvious. They can often be seen peering through window blinds or standing behind fences. If they could only understand how uninteresting our lives truly are, they might stop.

Welcome to the Jungle Asshole:

The Welcome to the Jungle asshole seems to think that everyone in your street can benefit from developing Amazonian survival instincts. He believes in this cause so whole-heartedly that this asshole will provide the street you live in with a dangerous, overgrown vegetation cesspit of its very own. The taller the grass and weeds the better for this asshole. Rather than do yard work of any kind they would rather live in the wild and share that dream with you. There is perhaps nothing like providing the world with an opportunity to have rats, snakes, spiders and every other type of vermin live as close as possible to our homes and to our children. If your child can't wrangle a snake on the way to school there is something missing in their lives really. To add that touch of class you can often see a few old soggy pizza boxes strewn about, and one to five old cars that have not moved since a November many years ago. The devaluation of the street is particularly pleasing for anyone that may be trying to sell a house at the time. Welcome to the Jungle assholes are usually there to stay, so it is probably best to avoid eye contact, and head out with a hefty tub of round-up after dark.

9)   Restaurant Assholes

The Booming Asshole:

Boom. Restaurant assholes are there for all restaurant goers to enjoy – like it or lump it, if you are in the vicinity of a booming asshole you will know all about it. They are loud! They truly believe themselves to be a genuine source of entertainment, and they seem to find it their duty here on earth to shout out a variety of topics. There are the jokes of course, these are never funny and we want them to never be funny. Any sign of any form of laughter no matter how faint from anywhere in the room will encourage boom boy to continue with a heightened fervor. There are many, many, many questions for the wait staff, and chances are our booming friends will have a multitude of particular preferences and no doubt some rare allergies.

An audience in a room is the hunting ground of the booming asshole. There is not much you can do here, just follow the basic rules; don't laugh, don't make eye contact, and take an aspirin if your eyes ache from all the rolling they have to do.

The Rude Asshole:

The rude asshole is often a mutation of the booming asshole. The rude asshole takes loud, annoying and inappropriate to a higher level. The rude asshole believes that wait staff simply must be punished at every opportunity. The rude asshole will always have an unpleasant restaurant experience. Nothing will be right; the waiter will be a veritable twit, the food will be awful, the table itself will be unsatisfactory and by God everyone will know about it. Of course the rude asshole can have two effects on wait staff. The first will be to make them so nervous/angry that the service will get rapidly worse. This is a serious play by the rude asshole. A competent, hardworking, perfectly nice person can actually be reduced to a moron. The second effect, and the one everyone would actually like to bear witness to, is the waiter fighting back. This can be done verbally, and there is nothing better than a rude asshole finding out publically that the offended waiter is super smart, articulate and gifted with equal doses of wit and sarcasm. Seeing a waiter out-joust an asshole is a dream we all can hope to see come true. A less evolved waiter or waitress may possibly take the physical route. That is clouting the asshole with a chicken leg, perhaps sloshing a nice hot soup into the assholes lap, or for the most theatrical of them all, throwing a glass of wine into their face, or on top of the assholes head. This is truly the stuff dreams are made of. It's more than likely though, that the rude asshole will encounter a smirking waiter. A smirk filled with the knowledge of what has been done to the assholes food before it left the kitchen. Rude assholes are very likely to have their food given special attention. A nightmare scenario; completely deserved.

10)   Facebook Assholes

The Too Cool for School Asshole:

The closeted Facebook users. These are the ones who constantly make fun of Facebook and ridicule anyone and everyone for using it yet are keenly aware of all the comings and goings of everyone on their friends list. It's ironic that they carry such negative feelings for something they apparently can't stay away from. They suffer from a deep seated self-loathing brought on by their inability to ignore that what they hate most.

The Dramatic Asshole:

This asshole is drama royalty. The world is really against these assholes, apparently, because terrible things happen to them every day and each and every one of them are posted on Facebook. Their Facebook status often reads something like these:

The "For the love of God give me some attention post"

Sometimes I feel so alone in the world...(sigh)

The "I matter here so very much, don't I?" post

I'm not going to be on FB for the next 10 days. I need some alone time to find myself. However you can still text me, call me, email me or come by my house unexpectedly if you want to.

The "Please see my half-assed self-improvement" post

I had an affirmation today: I realized I wasn't put on this earth to worry about greedy, selfish, mean people. I'm pretty and smart and awesome and I was put here to do much bigger things with my life. I don't care what ANYONE thinks! "Like" this if you think that's a good move.

The "Poor me" post!

I'm just so sick and tired of people that think just because a person is caring, nice and goes down on them 3 hours after they've met it means they are easy and can be taken for granted...

Oh the drama! Facebook audibly groans each time the drama asshole has an issue. Hey asshole, want a tissue?

The Neophobe Asshole:

Webster's online dictionary defines Neophobe as "The word you've entered isn't in the dictionary. Click on a spelling suggestion below or try again using the search bar above." So I said fuck them and kept looking for the answer I wanted. Dictionary.com defines Neophobe as "A tendency to dislike anything new; fear of novelty." Yea, there ya go....fear of change.

Change is nothing like a holiday for these assholes. Changes to Facebook are a personal insult and world rocking, traumatic event to this group of individuals. We've all heard it;

"WHAT??? I have to convert to Timeline now?? What the fuck?!?!?! How can this be happening to me? How can this free, completely voluntary social media time waster fuck me like this??? It is puzzling beyond all measure, and it is so catastrophic that they may very well never use Facebook again! Except, they use it more; to bitch about it more. They may even be inclined to start an anti-Facebook Facebook page. They are unpredictable and potentially revolutionary once they are forced into new arenas. This spiffing example of assery NEEDS change as much as it hates change. Without it, things would only stay the same and this asshole would get itchy about something else anyway.

The Passive Aggressive Asshole:

This has got to be one of my absolute least favorites. These attention starved marvels have an issue or problem they're just DYING to talk about but don't want to take the direct approach so instead they choose to post a vague, beat around the bush, mumbo jumbo of words that just BEGS people to ask "OMG, what's wrong? Is everything OK?" Something like this, "SO over it!"...or this, "I just wanna crawl into a hole and die..." Christ! Just spit it out or keep it to yourself. It's not Therapybook, it's Facebook. Put some frickin pictures up of what you ate for lunch like everyone else. At least there's no guessing involved in that.

The "Who Cares" Asshole:

Our "who cares" asshole simply doesn't care! They comment as such, 'who cares'. They don't care. Not one bit. Except that they care enough to write 'who cares'. This is an oddity as perplexing as it is irritating.   Facebook has a fascinating collection of assholes that just don't care. They say so. They are a measurable quantity. They make it known that they don't care. They could remain stealthy by not commenting at all, but no, no, no, they must tell us that they don't care, they must make it known that they don't care, they must. They must. They must. Or else who will know what they don't care about?

The Loose Cannon Asshole:

Know your audience. The cover of this book has the word "ASSHOLE" emblazoned across the front. Anyone looking at this cover will either be A) intrigued or B) offended. Either one of those groups will probably jump to the conclusion that there is more profanity to be found within the pages of this literary masterpiece. I wanted to have profanity in this book because the subject matter makes me cranky and when I'm cranky, I cuss. It's my one weakness (aside from women, gambling, video games, pornography, iCarly and mild narcotics). I feel comfortable using profanity within the book because I used profanity on the cover. Anyone offended by the cover but continues to read anyway shouldn't get mad at me. Had I named the book "Don't be a Poopy Head" and then laced the insides with foul-mouthed trash, that would be a jerk move on my end.

The Loose Cannon Asshole NEVER knows its audience. They will post all about their sexual escapades, drug induced nights on the town (with pictures) and any other personal crap they find worth sharing with no regard whatsoever for their moms, little sisters, teachers, etc. who look on in shocked horror from the glowing screens of their own PC's. I didn't even mention all the potential future employers that will see how many Jager shots you can suck out of a transvestite's navel. Who WOULDN'T want to hire you after seeing THAT? It's awesome that you're wild and crazy and don't stop on MY account because that shit's entertaining as Hell, but if you care about your relative's delicate sensibilities and your own future house payments, take it easy. Censor yourself once in a while. Show some self-respect. But still text me the pics. I can take it.

Asshole Code:

This asshole has mastered the art of modern shorthand. Words are not required. Not real ones anyway. Here is an example:

-RU cmin ovr 2nite?

Luv 2. Wut tme?

-9ish. Mt u @ my houz

Gr8. C U thn.

Text speak is code for the illiterate. If you can't read it, it seems to be because you are not supposed to. You don't have the cool factor, so be gone with you. You with your fancy high school diploma.

You don't know it yet, you little trendsetters, but you are all actually a symbol yourselves...This one → (_*_)

The Asshole "Situation":

I'm talking about the slew of idiots whose profile pictures consist of them taking a picture of themselves, shirtless and usually in a dirty bathroom with embarrassing things in the background like fungal creams and dirty underwear. I'm focusing more on the guys here because you just look so stupid in these pics. Seriously. It doesn't matter if you're ripped or rolled, you look dumb. You have 1287 "friends" but not ONE person can take a picture of you? You have to do it yourself? If you're gay and you're trying to look it, by all means carry on. If you're not, you may want to rethink your strategy.

The Grim Poster:

There's no news like BAD news. That's the motto of the Grim Poster. They are firm believers in "misery loves company" so it's their passion to share their misery with everyone in Facebookland. Job losses, deaths, disturbing current events; everything is fair game for these party pooping, cereal pissing, parade raining good mood suckers of the web. Don't they understand that Facebook is merely an outlet to show the world how much better your life is going than everyone else's? People don't want gloom and doom. If that were the case they would focus more on the real world around them. Life sucks. Life on Facebook is one happy illusion after another. Celebrate it!

The Reposted Asshole:

"I know some of you will repost this but most won't"...please. First, don't try to guilt or peer pressure me in to reposting something I really don't care about. You love God. You hate cruelty to animals. You're against a certain political party. Those are all righteous things; just don't make me feign interest to promote your cause. I just found a hilarious e-card about drinking wine and it's gonna bring the world to its knees with its sheer comedic brilliance and originality.

Assholes just love to create a chain of reposts. Not the cool viral stuff. Noooo, the stuff that says 'repost if you love your children', - hey asshole, go hang out with your kid, get off Facebook.

The other kind you see are the Faceboobs that always seem 6 months behind everyone else. They barrage your wall with pics and meme's that stopped being funny ages ago. They forget the first rule of comedy...

...timing.

The bathroom self-pic…when none of your 5000 friends knows how to work a camera…

Inspiration Intermission #4

I got nothing. Just read this:

You Gotta be Kidney, Right?!?!

Hey remember when I told you about the couple who gave the waiter a $5000 tip? That was really cool right? Well hold onto your butts because the woman I'm about to tell you about gave a total stranger a piece of herself. Get your mind out of the gutter asshole, it wasn't THAT.

A kindergarten teacher in Texas found out one day that one of her students, a five year old boy, had a dad who was in desperate need of a kidney transplant. The father had recently gone to the hospital for a transplant but the kidney he was supposed to get turned out to be diseased. Without a viable transplant he had to go to dialysis three times a week. That in itself sucked, but it was far better than the alternative.

The teacher just couldn't fathom the idea of the boy, who also had an older brother, growing up without their dad so she decided to give the man one of her kidneys. She gave the man one of her kidneys. I'm saying it twice because a gift of that magnitude deserves that kind of special attention. She gave a stranger a second chance at life and gave those kids their father back. Wow. Just...wow.

The thought of giving organs away kind of makes you reconsider that $5000 tip now doesn't it?

Hang in there people, we're in the home stretch now.

11) Assholes through Email

I'ma Put a CAP in Your Ass:

They cap you, they cap me, and they cap total strangers. They are the shouty, rude (or just oblivious) emailing asshole. These assholes make simple emails damn near unreadable or at least suck the desire out of you to even WANT to read them. They have such important and time sensitive data to give you in email form that they must use all caps; they must use exclamation points to within an inch of our lives and they must, simply must, receive acknowledgement that you received their ridiculous piece of bullshit. Here's the deal, it makes it very hard to read AND IT MAKES IT APPEAR THAT YOU'RE YELLING ABOUT EVERYTHING!!! If you are indeed yelling, firstly, fuck off. Secondly, I don't hear with my eyes so it's kind of pointless. Thirdly, fuck off. If you're not yelling, it immediately makes you look stupid. If this is how you're sending your resume to potential employers, it's no wonder why you haven't had a job in three years.

Sadly for these assholes, they generate an opposing asshole. The asshole sends an email using excessive caps, and the recipient becomes the trashing asshole. The trashing asshole ensures your email is deleted, that it is ignored, but before that happens they will ensure that it is the focus of interoffice scorn, and that you, are labeled 'that asshole'. Please asshole, say it nicely. Your emails are hyperactive, unprofessional, and an act of seemingly deliberate assholery.

The "Put A Spell On Me" Asshole:

Spell check. It's free. It's automatic. It's included in just about every form of electronic data entry. So HOW are there still so many people sending texts and emails with misspelled words??? Seriously, I really want to know. Are they always in a hurry? Are they doing it on purpose just to annoy the crap out of everyone? Maybe they don't know how to spell? Well that's the beauty of spell check. It spells FOR you. Right click on the word in question and it even gives you suggestions. How easy is that? See, here's the deal; when you type something out and the words are all resting comfortably on a sea of bright red lines, that's not the program complimenting you on a well written piece; it's telling you it's all jacked up. Fix it!

If you are lucky enough to be in regular email contact with an illiterate asshole, you have really hit the jackpot and I actually want to be you. When these assholes email you, you just know that at some point they will make you smile. A former manager of mine spent 3 months signing off her business emails as 'Kind Retards'. Ahhh, I just couldn't tell her. It was just too good! I know that makes me a selfish asshole, but I don't care. I've already admitted to being a major asshole myself. Only the biggest assholes think everyone ELSE is an asshole so that makes me the king.

On another occasion I received an email from a client who wanted a website designed. They sold fantasy birthday parties for kids. As you can imagine, I had the biggest smile on my big dumb face when I received a request to build a website to be named 'Fatnasty Birthday Parties'. It took all of my self-control and some I borrowed from other people not to buy that URL for the company. Sigh.

Color Me an Asshole:

Some folks seem to think emails are the perfect place to highlight their artistic skills. It's not. I'm talking about the people who must spend just oodles of valuable productivity hours customizing their sentences with different colors and fonts and an annoyingly excessive use of bold and underlining. The senders are usually micromanaging middle management types who think it is necessary to over explain everything to their underlings. If you think I'm so stupid that I can't ascertain the important bits of an email using normal text and properly structured sentences then why on Earth did you hire me? Or are you just so rife with free time that manipulating all those little drop down boxes means nothing to you? Whatever the reason, quit it. Opening an email like that doesn't make me pay closer attention; it makes me delete it faster just based on its obnoxiousness.

Author Asshole:

Here I'm referring to the people that feel the need to write out every detail in their detail oriented minds for the simplest of things. I appreciate the fact that there are no grammatical errors or misspelled words but a response to the question, "Wanna hit Applebee's for lunch today?" should not necessitate a 2000 word essay in response. Yes or no, bitch. Yours is not the only email I'm reading today.

Getting an email of this magnitude from anyone outside of work has an easy solution. Delete and deny. "What email? I never got an email from you." Work situations can be more difficult, especially if it's coming from someone in an authority position because then you HAVE to read it. Luckily your skimming skills become quite effective when you've done it long enough. The key words pop out at you like some sixth sense allowing you to get to the frickin point, without wasting all afternoon reading this person's "next great American novel".

Keep emails concise and to the point. You're killing those on the other end.

12)   Assholes on the Phone

The Elevator Asshole:

I find it hard to write about these schmucks because of the homicidal thoughts they cause me to have. On a cell phone...in an elevator. Nothing chaps my ass the way these assholes do. There is nothing like listening to the following conversation while trapped in the confined quarters of an elevator with this:

"Are you there? I can't hear you! Hello. Yeah, yeah I'm in an elevator. What? Hello? The reception is really bad in here. Hello! I'll call...I'll call...I'll call you back..."

Or if there's a hint of a cell signal, this:

"Hey, I'm in an elevator. WHAT??? You're breaking up. OK, you're back. No I can talk now. Listen what's your status on the Grainer account? Hello? What's that? One more time. I only caught the last part of that. No, now's fine. There you are. Can you hear me? So I was asking what your status was on the...hello? Oh, ok. So listen..."

Do you know this asshole? Are you this asshole? If you are please, please, punch yourself in the face.

You're in a FUCKING ELEVATOR with 7 other people!! Hang the fuck up and call back in 15 seconds. Is it so hard? You can't hear anyway. You're moving vertically in a steel box, of COURSE you can't hear. You weren't meant to, and in the mean time you're THIS close to getting a Judo chop to the Adam's apple. You seriously don't think there's anything wrong with what you're doing right now? If that's the case I hope you're on the way to see a behavioral therapist because your behavior is in serious need of some therapy.

I'd like to Deposit One Asshole:

Cell phone users at the bank. You can bank on one of these assholes showing up. Like you need them. Going to the bank is a horrible exercise in itself. But when an asshole shows up to compound the situation things go from bad to worse real fast. You're in the bank and you hear this:

"What time will you be home?. Because don't forget that Bob and Priscilla are coming over for dinner. I told them we are having duck. So we're having duck. What? Don't swear at me. It's just a duck. What do you mean you've never cooked a duck? Just pretend it's a chicken. God. Why do you always have to make such a big deal...what, what. What did you say? What do you mean you won't be home tonight? Who's going to cook the duck? What? Oh, you always do this....."

As if the day isn't bad enough, now you're left wondering for the rest of your life if the duck ever happened. Who the Hell eats duck anyway? Who are you, Thurston Howell III?? Please, all you cell phone talking assholes in the bank, just stop it. No one should ever be allowed to say duck in a bank. One, you are likely to get arrested, which you deserve because you are an asshole, and two, stop talking. You're in a bank. It is like a library for money. Your silence is expected.

Go Sell Asshole Somewhere Else:

Telemarketers. There is nothing worse than an asshole getting his hands on your phone number. An asshole really believes that phoning you in your home to try to sell you something is a great idea. These are worse than door to door sales people. They are worse because they are sinister. They have no face. They know when you're home, and they know you well enough to get you irate within seconds. These assholes are just assholes. Never is the perfect time for them to call. Calling you to bother you about things you don't want is only phase one of this asshole's act, phase two occurs when you say no. You may slam down the phone, you may politely say goodbye, you may refer to the fact that you are registered on the "do not call" list (which sounds a lot more intimidating than it really is) and you may even thank them very much but still say no thank you, but then comes phase two. They call back. They always call back. They call back to point out the error of your ways, to give you another chance to buy that timeshare in Orlando. They really are dedicated to pissing you off. Please stop calling me. You can call everyone else. Just not me.

Asshole Can You Spare a Dime?:

These are cruel and unusual phone sales people. They don't want you to buy anything, no, no, no. They want you to give. To contribute. To help. They are phoning you with a unique and special offer to save the whales, save the children, eradicate the Ebola virus, grow bamboo for the pandas or build a path of safe passage for garden snails. They are taking the time out of their day to find you and offer you a road straight to heaven. All you need to do is give them your credit card number so they can extract money from you without causing you any inconvenience at all. This is philanthropy at its finest. Except it's not. People, if you believe in a cause then please BELIEVE in a cause, and then inspire ME to believe in your cause. When you call unannounced during dinner to ask me for money simply because it's your crappy, part time job, you disappoint me. You know who gets it? The ASPCA, that's who. Holy crap. Everyone's seen their commercials. They're famous now. They're like emotional warfare. You're hanging out with your buds watching a game when all of a sudden you're pummeled with images of three legged puppies and one eyed kittens while Sarah McLachlan ever so gently rips your heart through your chest with that Angel song. Before you know it you're sobbing like a baby in the fetal position and throwing twenties at the TV and yelling "make it stop, make it stop!" That's how you do it people! Follow their lead. They should be the richest not-for-profit organization in the world by now. Calling me to help raise money for a cause you can barely pronounce yourself and know nothing about outside of your prepared script and sounding like Ben Stein doesn't exactly make me want to write a check.

Inspiration Intermission #5

Let's end this bitch on a high note, shall we?

Don't Be Crude.

There was an oil spill on MY beach. A dirty, stinky oil spill. Now oil is the work of assholes. From acquiring it, to transporting it, to selling it. Oil is an entire industry of assholes. We all know this, don't we?

But when it lands on a beach, it brings out the asshole in everyone. No one can believe what these assholes have done. How did these assholes let this happen? Why is our Government full of assholes not doing anything about this? Who the hell are these assholes? And of course, well, which one of you assholes is going to clean this mess up?

Yup, the beach becomes asshole central. At this particular oil spill there was a very coordinated effort to clean the beach. You had to sign up, you had to commit to a certain number of hours, and you even had to wear a special white plastic onesie. (Don't even get me started on that). Now, the people that were co-coordinating this operation were turning people away in droves. That's not a typo. They were TURNING AWAY people who wanted to VOLUNTEER to clean up OIL from water, sand, birds, discarded beer bottles, medical waste.... The reasons being:

They could not to commit to a solid week of work

They did not pass the medical questions (one boy had broken his arm 3 years ago!)

Some were too old

Some were too young

It was bizarre, but this is supposed to inspire, so wait for it.

As it happened, a couple that had been turned away from being allowed to help, because they were over the ripe old age of 55, owned a fast food franchise. So, they decided to help in the only way they could see. They delivered every volunteer working on the beach (at least 1000 people, maybe more) a meal and a drink, as well as a voucher for free food for a week for them and their family. It was the biggest convoy of vehicles swarming to the beach to deliver food. The Red Cross would have been proud! To see the face of the director as the couple that she had rudely turned away, handed her a lunch, drink and voucher, with a smile. This was a precious moment, a shining light of joy amongst a filthy oily beach.

V.   CONCLUSION:

As I wrote this book one question consistently popped in my head over and over again. Why? Why do people act this way? The answer I came up with once everything was all said and done is "because we're all only human". Nobody's perfect. Yes, not even me (as hard as that was to come to grips with). My belief is that every person who appears to be just a complete and total asshole is three questions away from our understanding, acceptance, acknowledgement and ultimately, our friendship. What I mean by that is most of the time we'll unabashedly label someone an asshole for doing (insert example here) but if we took 10 minutes to find out what was going on in their heads, more often than not we would be really surprised at how easy it is for this random "asshole" to turn back into a person we can relate to on a human level. I would be willing to bet that it would happen EVERY time. It's just easier and, let's face it, more satisfying to label THEM assholes so WE can feel better about ourselves for a moment. Tolerance and understanding are the keys to acceptance and peace.

The list of reasons people act the way they do is as long and varied as the list of people that are still breathing. Reasons range from complete ignorance to lapses in judgment to mental illness. Everyone is different and we all have different sets of circumstances that have brought us to this moment in our lives. We can allow other people's actions to affect us in a negative way or we can work on being more tolerant and finding out the underlying reasons why people sometimes act the way they do. That guy that's weaving in and out of traffic, going 100 mph with no apparent regard for safety could be on the way to the hospital because he just found out his daughter may have only moments to live. Maybe that girl you know on Facebook with all the drama laden posts just feels she has no one else to really talk to and needs some moral support. Some people need more support than others. Maybe that's what's keeping her from suicide. Who knows?

When people make you crazy in life, just try to take some deep breaths, keep an open mind and heart and remember that the next time someone spots an asshole, it could very well be YOU!

-AV

Be a part of the revolution!!!

Have your voice heard and your story in my next book!

I think what I've put together here is a decent start but just that...a start. I want to hear what asshole examples YOU have. Send me the types of assholes you've had run-ins with or stories about situations you've had when you thought the other person was a total asshole and what you did. If I pick your story for the next book, I'll credit you with it and send you a free "Don't Be an Asshole" t-shirt.

Send your stories/comments/suggestions to:

albert@dontbeanassholebook.com

Visit us on the web at:

www.dontbeanassholebook.com

Or on Facebook:

http://on.fb.me/RpYn8x

Together we can rid the world of assholes!

(not really, but I don't want to take the wind out of your sails)

New "B" vs. Old "B"

Step 1 – Don't be an asshole